BIG joke mash-up!

Silver Dolphin

This book is all you need to fill your days with joking joy!

Record and rate your pranks in the section at the back, and remember: practice turns a flop into a **triumph!**

Absolutely not for anyone who's old enough to know better!

RULES OF PRANKING

A true pranker will follow these basic—but important—rules!

1 Never play a prank on a complete stranger— you never know how they might react!

2 Pick your subjects with care and consideration— pranking your 90-year-old neighbor is **not** funny. (Pranking your best friend *is* funny.)

3 Most pranks require practice. Make sure you've perfected the prank before you spring the surprise!

4 If you play practical jokes, you have to be prepared to be pranked back. Make sure you can see the funny side!

5 Spread the fun! If you keep pranking the same person, your pranks will cease to be surprising!

6 Make sure your subjects have no allergies before carrying out pranks involving food.

7 If your prank is messy, clean up once it's over.

What are you waiting for? →

R U dedicated to pRaNkiNg?

Check the **boxes**, and then **add up** your score.

A day without pranking is . . .

☐ like a day without TV. **(2)**

☐ like any other day. **(1)**

☐ not worth getting out of bed for. **(3)**

Which of these could you not live without?

☐ joke book **(2)**

☐ fake bug **(3)**

☐ handkerchief **(1)**

Your sister is about to go on a date and you notice a rather attractive booger hanging from her nose. Do you?

☐ Tell her straight away. **(1)**

☐ Keep it zipped and watch the booger boogie! **(3)**

☐ Offer a tissue, and let her do the math. **(2)**

Add up your scores, and then turn the book **upside down** (if you can . . .)

Doodle some **hairs** sprouting from the **wart.**

It's a **pranking** world!

Join two words to make place names, and write them in the signs.

Booger — wart
Wiffy — fluff
Putrid — spew
Dusty — ache
Zitty — scab
Nose — burp

One from here

One from here

4 **revolting** *delicious* pizza toppings

tomato and

and sausage

tuna and

and ham

Why did the **tomato** go to **Italy?**

It wanted **a pizza** the **action!**

Whose cat did that?

Fake puke is easy to make and great for livening up boring family parties, or just annoying your big sister.

You will need:
- craft glue
- plastic wrap
- an old magazine
- a cookie or cracker

First crush up the cookie. Be sure to have a good mix of chunky pieces and fine, crumbly pieces.

Place the plastic wrap flat on the magazine. Squirt a blob of glue onto the plastic wrap, and then sprinkle the crushed cookie on top.

Leave for at least a day, and then gently peel the fake puke from the plastic wrap.

WARNING

Never put your puke on clothing, fancy furnishings, or anywhere it could leave a stain!

What did the sausage say to the bacon?

I HAM so pleased to MEAT you!

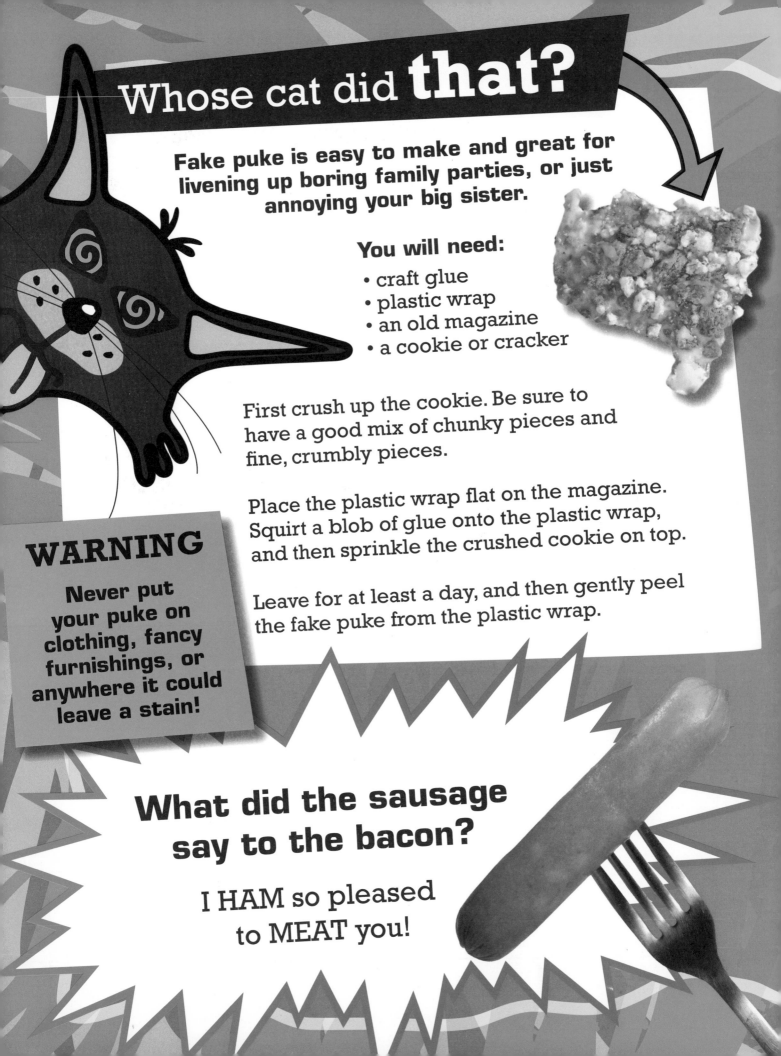

EEEEK!

Where does a skunk do its washing up?

In the kitchen STINK!

Toilet **TROUBLE** PART 1

Make nature's call a moment to remember with this perfect prank!

When no one is looking sneak into the bathroom and remove the roll of toilet paper.

Using a hole punch and a piece of paper, make a good helping of paper dots. Roll out about six sheets of toilet paper and scatter dots on the paper until you are two sheets from the end.

Next, carefully roll the paper back up and hook it on the toilet-paper holder. When your subject pulls at the roll, they'll find themselves showered in tiny dots!

NAME:

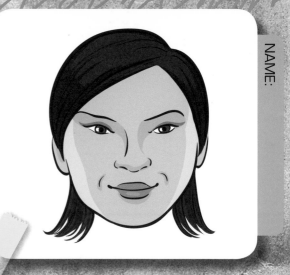

NAME:

Doodle on disguises

NAME:

Give them names, if you must.

NAME:

NAME:

NAME:

NAME:

NAME:

NAME:

NAME:

NAME:

What did the **kettle** say when the **pot** lost his **temper?**

Just SIMMER down!

How do you make a hotdog stand?

Hide its chair!

BIG FOOT!

This prank is perfect for hot summer days.

Begin the prank by telling your subject you've read about how, in the summer, the heat makes people's feet grow bigger. Ask them if they've ever heard this, and then change the subject. Next day, take a rolled–up handkerchief or sock and stuff it in the toes of your subject's shoes. Let the laughs roll in as they think their feet have ballooned!

DUH!

Spaghetti Trees!

One of the most famous April Fool's pranks of all time was on British TV over 50 years ago. The news show *Panorama* showed farmers in Switzerland picking strings of spaghetti from their "Spaghetti trees." This caused a sensation with viewers all over the country phoning in and asking where they could buy the trees so they could grow their own!

5 excellent uses for a
whoopee cushion

1 Slip it under the cushion of your dad's chair.

2 Give it a squeeze just as everyone sits down for a nice family lunch.

3 How about ripping a fart at the dentist's office?

4 Or leaving it under a cushion in your sister's bedroom?

5 Prank your pal by leaving a cushion on his seat at the movie theater—it'll be so dark, he'll never see it coming!

What can you give and keep at the same time?

A cold!

What's a fisherman's favorite musical instrument?

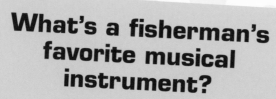

The cast-a-nets!

Why did the traffic lights blush?

Because the trucks saw them changing!

What's the best snack to eat on a roller coaster?

F-RISE and dip!

What do you call a man with a car on his head?

Jack!

What jungle creature does Tarzan keep in his car?

Windshield vipers!

How did the gnome get indigestion?

By goblin his food!

How did the tap dancer break his leg?

He fell in the sink!

Secret codes

If you want to be the best pranker, you need to keep your secrets safe, and the best way to do this is to create your own code.

Try using this back to front alphabet. Instead of **A**, you write **Z**, instead of **B**, you write **Y**, and so on.

A	B	C	D	E	F	G	H	I	J	K	L	M
Z	Y	X	W	V	U	T	S	R	Q	P	O	N

N	O	P	Q	R	S	T	U	V	W	X	Y	Z
M	L	K	J	I	H	G	F	E	D	C	V	A

Instead of letters you could use shapes, numbers, or a mix of all three.

Try creating your own secret prank codes.

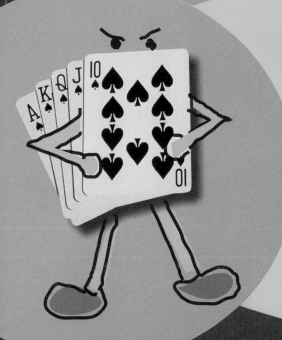

What did the dice say when the cards refused to shuffle?

I'LL DEAL WITH YOU LATER!

Doctor, Doctor! I think I'm a yo-yo!

How do you feel?

Sometimes I'm up, and sometimes I'm down!

ARGH!

Freaky finger!

Tell your subject you've found something interesting and ask them to open the box. Laugh out loud as your subject shrieks at the sight of your festering finger!

Find some cotton balls (enough to fill most of the box), dab them with dark red paint, and leave them to dry.

Find a small gift box, and cut a hole in the bottom—large enough to stick your finger through.

Cup the box in your hand, placing your middle finger through the hole. Pad out the box with the cotton balls. Put the lid on the box.

Offer the box to your friends, and wiggle your finger as they lift the lid!

Name
MASH-UP

Write your name, then mash it up by writing
it backwards or switching the letters around!

Your name:

- - - - - - - - - - - - - - - - - - - -
Mash it!
- - - - - - - - - - - - - - - - - - - -

Your friend's name:

- - - - - - - - - - - - - - - - - - - -
Mash it!
- - - - - - - - - - - - - - - - - - - -

**Now try mashing up
your friends' names!**

Another friend's name:

- - - - - - - - - - - - - - - - - - - -
Mash it!
- - - - - - - - - - - - - - - - - - - -

And another friend's name:

- - - - - - - - - - - - - - - - - - - -
Mash it!
- - - - - - - - - - - - - - - - - - - -

And another friend's name:

- - - - - - - - - - - - - - - - - - - -
Mash it!
- - - - - - - - - - - - - - - - - - - -

And another friend's name:

- - - - - - - - - - - - - - - - - - - -
Mash it!
- - - - - - - - - - - - - - - - - - - -

Gasp in wonder as plain old Jon Scott becomes Noj Ttocs!

And another friend's name:

_____

Mash it!

_____

And another friend's name:

_____

Mash it!

_____

And another friend's name:

_____

Mash it!

_____

And another friend's name:

_____

Mash it!

_____

And another friend's name:

_____

Mash it!

_____

So many friends. You rock!

_____

Mash it!

_____

Hello there! Noj by name, Ttocs by nature.

Bugs on string

Plastic bugs are so much fun and are guaranteed to bring joy wherever they go. Pump up the pranking potential by tying black thread to the bug Place your bug where your subject can't miss it, hide, and then pull the cord and watch the fun unfold.

Practice making the bug scamper quickly (quick pull), slither slowly (slow pull), or jolt forward (lots of quick, short pulls).

arrghhh!

arrghhh!

eeewWW!

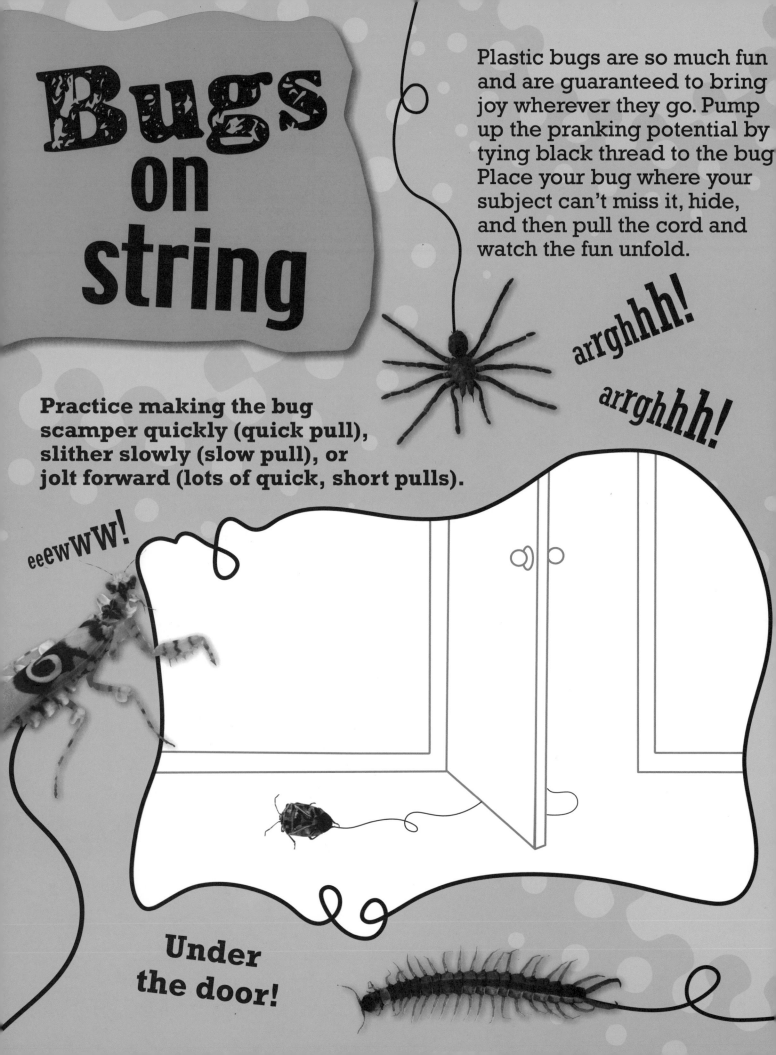

Under the door!

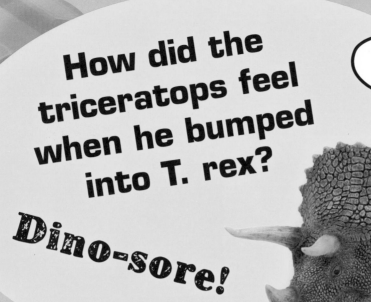

How did the triceratops feel when he bumped into T. rex?

Ouch!

Dino-sore!

The **DO NOTHING** prank

Here's a way to prank your pals by doing absolutely NOTHING.

A couple of days before April 1st, tell your pal you've heard of some really amazing April Fool's pranks. A little later, say you've thought up the most awesome prank ever, but refuse to share it. The next day, say you're just trying to decide who to pull the prank on. When April 1st comes, do nothing, but every time you see your pal smirk, look the other way, or do anything to look suspicious—for example, keep looking at their bag in a way that suggests you put something in it or you are about to! All the while, do nothing—the prank is that your pal spent the day thinking they were about to be pranked!

Yummy Gummy

Try these pranks and check each one when you've completed it. Then give it a thumbs up if you would do it again or a thumbs down if it was a major fail.

Gummy worms make great pranking tools. Make your folks a surprising snack by taking a nice big apple and making two or three holes in it. Let the apple stand for a couple of hours so the holes go nice and brown, then poke gummy worms into the holes and put the apple back in the fridge or fruit bowl. You'll worm your way into their hearts with this one!

Job done!

Oh, Boo!
There's No Shampoo!

Take a bottle of shampoo, remove the lid, and place a piece of plastic wrap over the lip. Put the lid back on. When the next person goes to wash their locks, they'll wonder why the shampoo is stuck in the bottle!

Job done!

Pasta Prank

Next time your family has spaghetti, keep a few of the strands and let them get cold. When no one is looking, take your brother's or dad's shoes, remove the laces, and put them somewhere safe. Carefully replace the laces with the spaghetti. Alternatively, use strawberry or liquorice laces for an even tastier trick!

Dumb Drink

Open a can of cola, drink it, and replace the liquid with cold soup. Offer your friend a drink, opening one for yourself at the same time so they think they hear the can opening. Watch in wonder as they slurp their souper surprise!

The **weirdest** thing I've ever seen was . . .

Did you see that?

at home ○   at school ○   at my friend's house ○   somewhere else ○

It was . . .

green ○   red ○   brown ○   something else ○

It made me . . .

laugh ○   barf ○

What was it?

....
....

Who else saw it?

....
....

When did the pencil stop talking?

When it got to the point!

The funniest thing I've ever seen looked like this . . .

Draw it here . . .

Why was the pony whispering?

Because he was a little horse!

SPRINGY SURPRISE!

Make opening a book a springy surprise!

Find a thick OLD book—that is, one that no one wants. If it's not yours, ASK first! A hardback book is best for this prank.

Draw a circle about 1.5 inches (3 cm) in diameter in the middle of the first page and use this as a guide to cut a hole about 80 pages deep. Cut several pages at a time, and use the hole you have cut to draw more cutting guides. Next, cut a strip of card about 6 inches (15 cm) long and a half inch (1 cm) wide. Fold the card back and forth every half inch (1 cm) to form a spring. Now cut a circle of card just bigger than the hole. Draw something gross like a bug or an eyeball on the disc, and stick it on the spring.

Fold the spring up, place it in the hole and carefully close the book. Hand the book to a friend, explaining that there is something completely fascinating on page 1. Point the book in their direction so they peer down. Then open the cover quickly to give them a springy surprise!

ARGH!

POINNNG!

Coffee Caper

In 2010, Starbucks® coffee shops pranked their customers by announcing two new cup sizes—an extra small 2-oz (50-ml) cup for customers who just wanted a sip, and a super-sized 128-oz (3.5-l) cup for extra-thirsty coffee lovers. The new big cups would be so big that customers could reuse them as lampshades or hats, while the sipping cups would make perfect paperclip holders!

What did the bed say when the curtains started crying?

Just pull yourself together!

The **most revolting** thing I've ever found:

1) Under my bed

In case you're interested, here's a picture of it.

2) In my bed

3) In my ear

Yes, it was that bad.

4) In my gym bag

Isn't that special?

5) Under my fingernails

6) At the bottom of my drink

This is 100 % exactly what it looked like.

7) In my closet

8) On my shoe

Still interested?

YIKES! My thumb BROKE!

This classic gag fools 'em every time!

1.
Bend the tops of both thumbs inward as far as you can.

2.
Place your thumbs together so that the bottom half of one thumb joins with the top half of the other.

3.
Wrap a forefinger around the "join" between the two thumbs.

4.
Raise the top half of your new thumb slowly and stifle your smirks as your friends are fooled into believing your thumb has broken in two!

TOP TIP! Practice different hand–finger combinations to perfect your prank!

OUCH!

Why did the fork get mad at the spoon?

Because it kept STIRRING things up!

How do you stop your phone battery from running out?

Hide its sneakers!

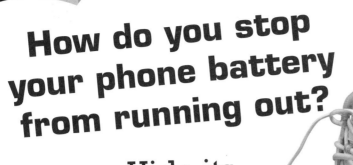

Hilarious Hankies!

Here's a great prank to play on an adult, but you'll need another adult to help.

Simply sew the corner of a handkerchief into the bottom of your subject's coat or pants pocket. Wait for them to sneeze or need to blow their nose, and then laugh your pants off as they fail to pull the pesky rag from their pocket!

THAT'S **NOT** FUNNY!

Heard any good jokes?

Write them down here before you forget them!

More "ho-ho-ho" than a sleigh full of Santas!

Move-it-around MAYHEM!

This hilarious gag is perfect to play on your sister or brother!

Sneak into your brother or sister's room and simply move things around a little. For example, switch the books on the bookshelf so they are in a different order, rearrange the contents of their drawers, or move their decorations or trophies onto a different shelf. They may not notice the changes at first, but if they do, deny all knowledge and make a mental note to make some more changes the following day!

After two days, reveal your prank or the confusion may make them completely crazy!

What goes HA! HA! BONK!

OOPS!

A man LAUGHING his head off!

Why did the toilet turn red?

Because it felt a little flushed!

SNOW JOKE

This is a classic prank—perfect for a rainy day!

Find a hole punch and a piece of paper, and punch as many holes as you can before you get completely bored or your wrist aches.

Find an umbrella, and open it slightly.

Pour the punched holes carefully into the umbrella, and tightly roll it back up.

Wait for your victim to open up their umbrella. Then roll on the floor laughing as they are showered with tiny paper dots!

SHOWER YOUR FRIENDS WITH PRANKS!

Hot head!

In 1995, a magazine called *Discover* claimed that a new species had been discovered in Antarctica. The brainy geeks told their readers that this fearsome creature had bones on its head that could become red hot, helping it to cut through snow and ice while chasing penguins! This hot news was, of course, nothing but nonsense!

Waiter, Waiter! There's a twig in my soup!

Then talk to our BRANCH manager!

HUH?!

chewy
challenge

Don't make your chewy **gooey!**

Start here

Name:  1

Name: 2

Name:  3

Name: 4

Name:  5

1) Start chewing your gum. While you're chewing, pick a numbered track and write your name next to the blob.

2) Once your gum is nice and soft, stick it on the blob and stretch it to the flag. Press it on the flag, and then stretch it back to the start. Then stretch it back to the flag, and then stretch it back to the start, and so on.

3) Keep going until your gum snaps. Record your lengths on the cup, and then challenge your friends.

Prank Talk

A sure-fire way to keep 'em clueless!

Fool your folks and keep your shenanigans secret by giving words alternative meanings. So, for example, instead of saying "boring," you could say "raspberry": **"Math class is SO raspberry today!"**

Word	Prank Language

What do you get if you put your pen in the freezer?
Iced ink?

Well, yes, you do smell, but that wasn't the answer!

Where did the worm leave its dog?

Tied to the caterPILLAR!

MAGGOT ATTACK!

It's so simple to fool your folks into believing their lovely fruit bowl has been invaded by insects!

Simply take an apple from the fruit bowl and, using a sharp pencil, make holes all around it. Leave the apple for a few hours so the holes get nice and brown. Then return the fruit to the bowl. Watch your mom howl in horror as she reaches for her favorite fruit!

SPLAT that?

Cut out these nasty splats . . .

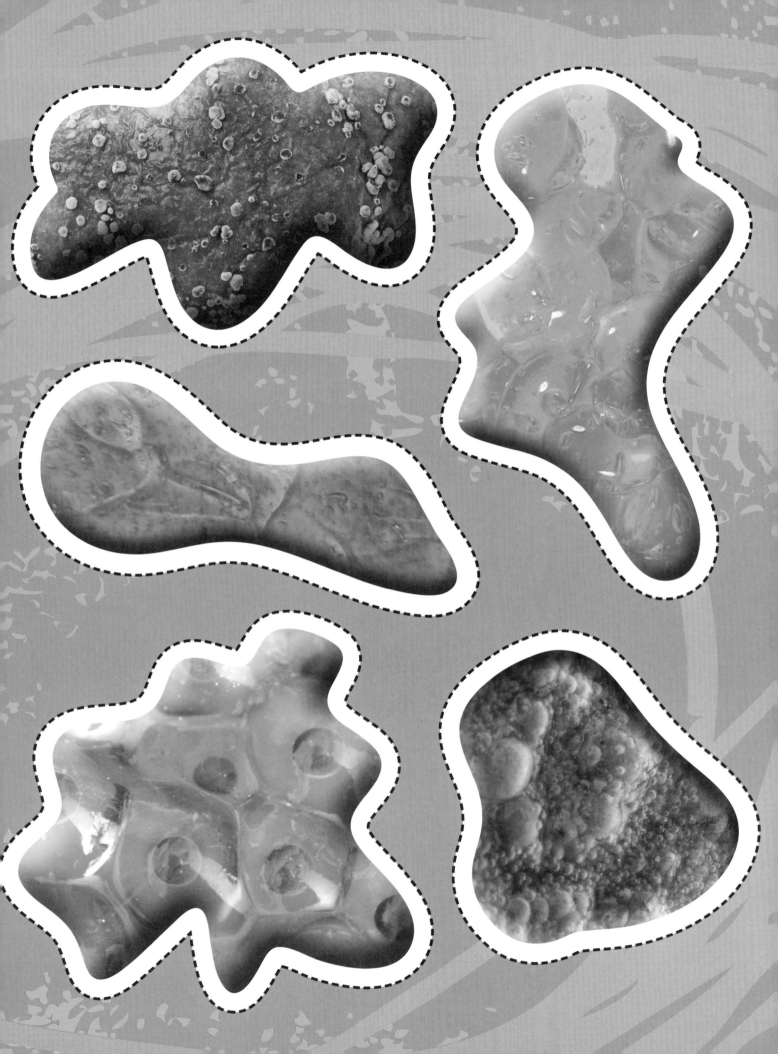

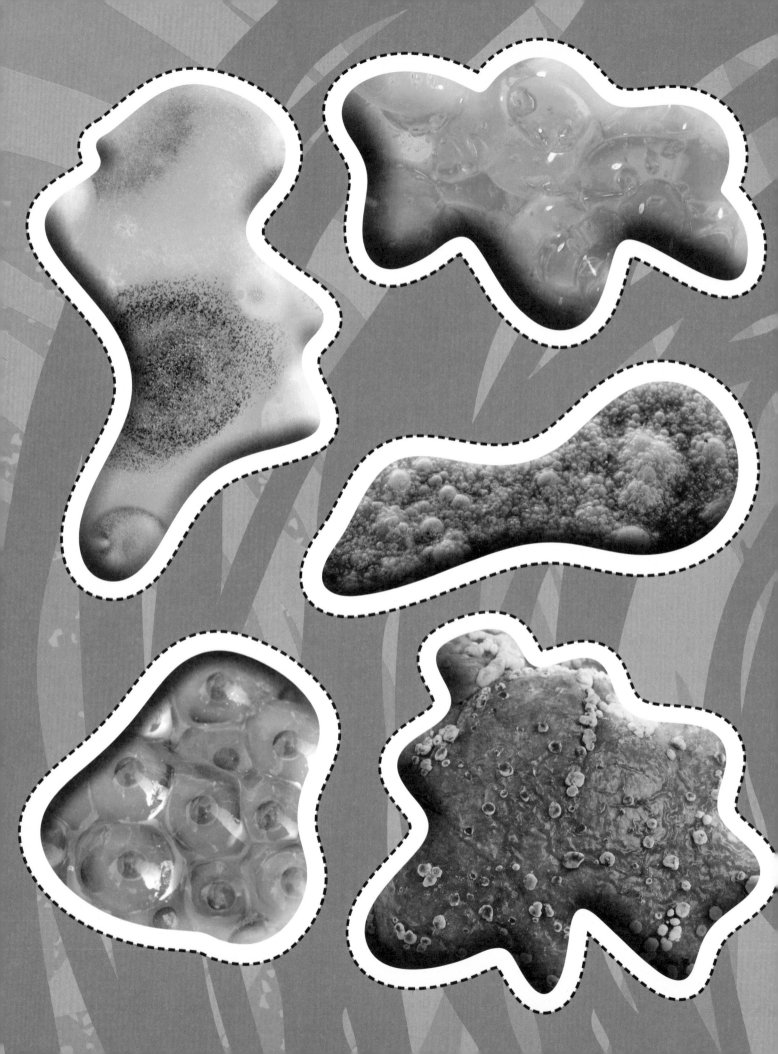

Why was the skeleton feeling lonely?

sniff!

Because he had NO BODY to play with!

real-life prank fact . . . real-life prank fact . . .

WHAT BARKING NONSENSE!

Animal Antics!

In 2010, Google took online pranking to a new level when it announced the "Translate for Animals" app. A special webpage announced that soon we'd be able to understand what our pets were saying with translations for dogs, chickens, sheep, and even tortoises!

TIME TROUBLE

Have your family in a spin by turning the clocks forward.

This prank is best performed on a day when everyone's home so the joke can be enjoyed by all! Get up early (difficult, but worth the trouble) and move as many clocks as you can forward by three hours. Stand back and watch the scramble as everyone thinks they are late for their important appointments!

ZOOOM

Why was the meatball tired?

Because it was **pasta** its bedtime!

YAWN!

What has a lot of heads and tails but no body?

A pocket full of change!

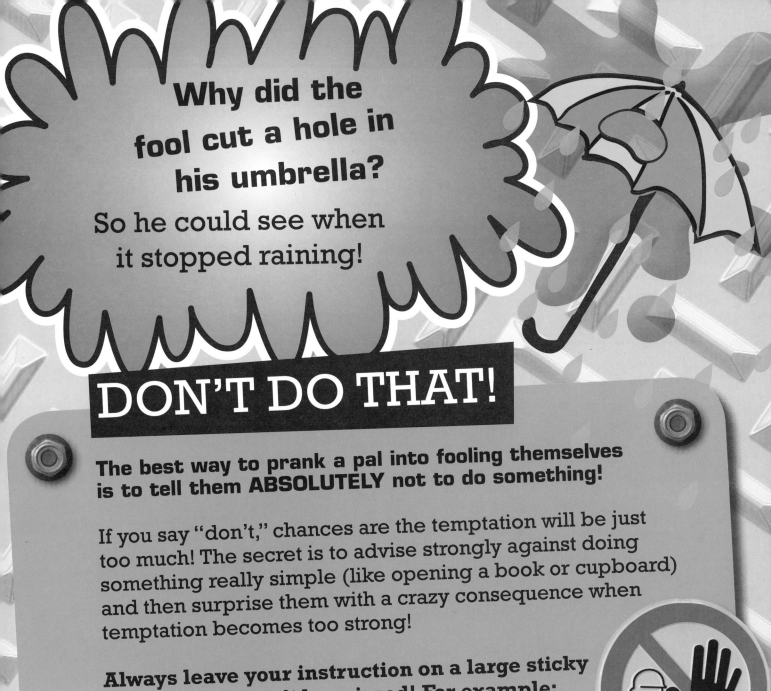

Why did the fool cut a hole in his umbrella?

So he could see when it stopped raining!

DON'T DO THAT!

The best way to prank a pal into fooling themselves is to tell them ABSOLUTELY not to do something!

If you say "don't," chances are the temptation will be just too much! The secret is to advise strongly against doing something really simple (like opening a book or cupboard) and then surprise them with a crazy consequence when temptation becomes too strong!

Always leave your instruction on a large sticky note where it can't be missed! For example:

"Do NOT open page 2!"
(Cover page 2 in hole-punch dots then carefully close the book.)

"This cupboard door must be kept CLOSED at all times!" (Hang plastic bugs and other freaky finds on the inside of the door frame.)

"Do not remove this newspaper!"
(Sneak a splat of homemade puke under the paper for a sickening surprise!)

sdrawkcab klat

Make your own backwards dictionary here. Write what you want to say, and then write it backwards.

Where's the best place to make a noise online?
The DIN-ternet!

CRASH

It doesn't add up!
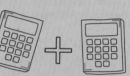
Cal Culator

Looks fishy to me . . .
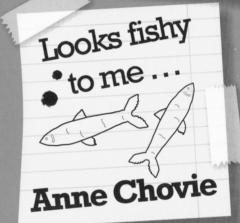
Anne Chovie

Moving MONEY!

Prank your pals as they make for the money!

Attach a coin to a long piece of black cotton thread, and place it on a table. Sit at the table with something light, like a piece of paper, covering the cotton thread trail and keeping your hand underneath the table, holding the end of the thread. Wait for your pal to join you at the table. Then, the moment he makes a dash for the cash, pull the cotton thread. Watch him jump out of his skin as the money escapes his greedy grasp!

BIG YAWN!

Send your pals to sleep with one of the simplest pranks ever!

Next time you're with a group of friends or at a family party, see if you can set off a train of tiredness by simply yawning! Yawn just a little at first, then after a minute or two, yawn a little louder and longer. Watch to see if anyone else yawns, and then yawn some more! Before long, the rest of the room will be sent into a snooze!

YAWN!!!!!!!

What did the frog order from the burger bar?

A CROAK and FLIES!

Rotten Rathers!

Would you rather . . .

Have triple math homework . . . or . . . **hug your best friend's sister?**

Eat your own nail clippings . . . or . . . **put your hands in a bag of raw fish?**

Put a ferret down your pants . . . or . . . **lick the bottom of your shoe?**

Wear your underwear over your clothes . . . or . . . **clean your sister's bedroom?**

Change your name to Doreen . . . or . . . **grow an extra ear?**

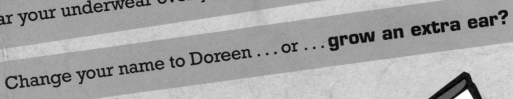

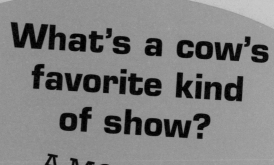

What's a cow's favorite kind of show?

A MOO-sical

What did the queen bee say when the worker bees started messing around?

Oh, do BEE-HIVE!

real-life prank fact . . . real-life prank fact . . .

Crazy color!

Years ago in Sweden, when all TV shows were shown in black and white, an expert announced that viewers could convert their TVs to color by simply pulling an old nylon stocking over the screen! Seems some silly Swedes thought it was a great idea and were surprised when the stocking netted no results!

Try these jokes on your friends, and then check one of the faces and rate the joke out of ten!

How do toads guide their boats through the mist?

With frog horns!

___/10

What gets bigger the more you take away from it?

A hole in the ground!

___/10

Why were the company directors yawning?

They were having a bored meeting!

___/10

Why did the gray pebble buy bright purple trousers?

He wanted to be a little bolder!

___/10

You will need these **donkeys.**

You don't know why.

But **YOU** will.

Cut them out!

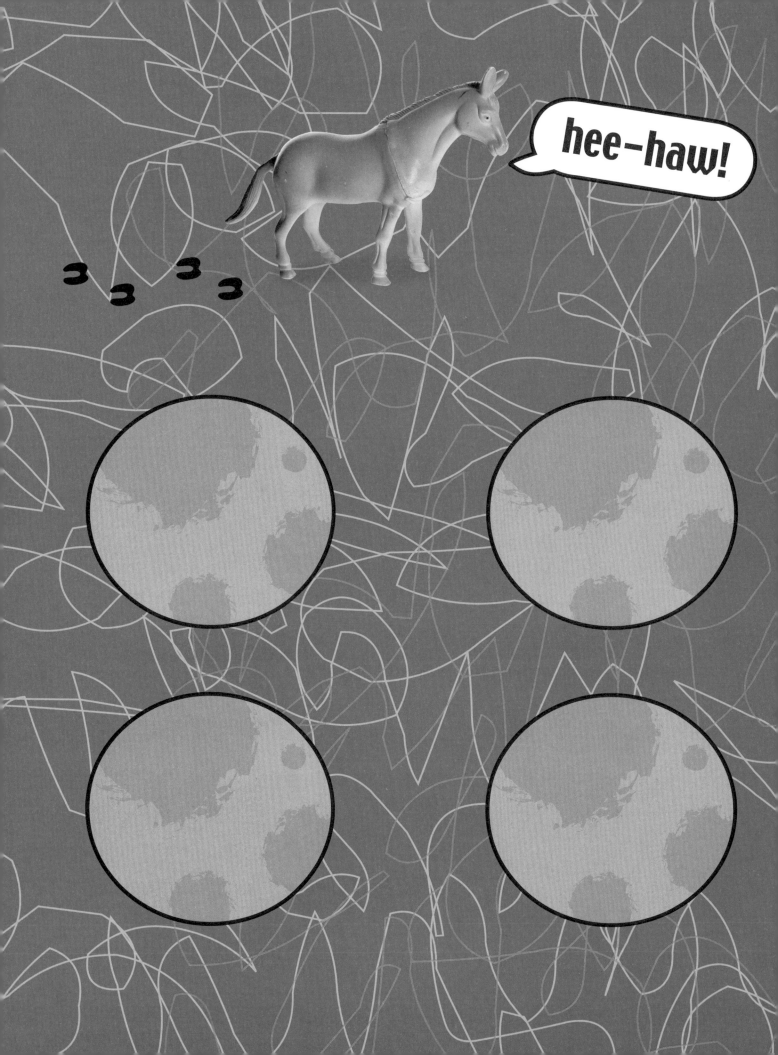

Just when you thought it couldn't get more exciting!

Never – ending (you will get) bored game.

START HERE

Forward 6

Forward 1

Finish!

EXCITING DONKEY RACE

No man has ever **WON** this game.
Will **you** be the first?

Back 7

Forward 3

Back 6

Forward 1

Back 3

Forward 4

Miss two turns!

Forward 5

Forward 6

7 Forward

1) Pick a donkey, cut it out, and place it on the start position.

2) Roll a die, and work your way around the track. How thrilling is that?

3) When you land on an instruction, you must do as it says (until you think of a better use of your time).

4) Keep going around the track until you land on the finish line.

Back 3

Forward 4

Back 2

Ha-ha, miss a turn!

Why didn't the snowman go to the disco?

Because he had tickets to the snow ball!

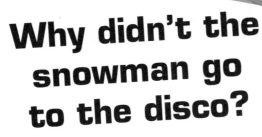

FAKE BOOGER!

Another cunning use of PVA glue—sure to delight friends and relatives alike!

You will need:

- craft glue
- an old magazine
- an old pencil
- green paint
- plastic wrap

Place the plastic wrap on the magazine. Squirt a blob of glue on the plastic wrap. Mix up a little green paint (or yellow, or both), and put a few drops on the glue blob. Use your pencil to mix the paint gently into the glue and create a nice booger shape. Leave it to dry for at least a day. Gently peel the booger off the plastic wrap.

What a PAIN!

Ever been told not to kick a ball in the house in case you **BREAK A WINDOW?** Prank your parents into believing you've done just that!

Take a piece of plastic wrap, and smooth it over a table or counter top. Using a black permanent marker, draw zigzag lines over the plastic wrap. Now, gently apply the plastic wrap to a handy window, grab your ball, and 'fess up!

PRO TIP

A window with curtains or blinds will work best as it will help hide creases in the plastic wrap!

Why did the monster eat the flashlight?

He wanted a light snack!

Try the jokes on your friends then check one of the faces and rate out of ten!

Why did the boy keep his iPod in the fridge?

Because he likes cool music!

What do cats eat for breakfast?

Mice Krispies!

Why do pirates keep soap under their hats?

To help wash them ashore!

What's green and refuses to join in games?

The incredible **sulk!**

What do you call a bee in a bell tower?

A humdinger!

___/10

Did you hear about the scientist who broke the law of gravity?

He got a suspended sentence!

___/10

Why do storks stand on one leg?

Because they'd fall over if they lifted both!

___/10

What's a shark's favorite sandwich?

Peanut butter and jellyfish!

___/10

There's nothing like being pranked when you're minding your own business!

When no one is looking, take the toilet roll from the bathroom. Replace it with a new roll until you are ready (so no one gets suspicious).

Unroll three sheets and put a few dots of glue on the third sheet. Roll it back up, press the glued area lightly, and leave it to dry.

Once the glue is totally dry, roll the paper back up and put it in the holder with the first two sheets left dangling. Wait for your subject to answer nature's call, then listen to them wail as they fail to unravel the roll!

FART!

Why did the brainiac eat her homework?

Because it was a piece of cake!

TEE HEE!

How do you make milk shake?

Say "BOO!"

BOO!

High-flyer!

Not all pranks go according to plan. In 1989, famous businessman Richard Branson had a hot-air balloon made to look like a flying saucer. The plan was to land in London's Hyde Park on April Fool's Day. Many motorists were fooled by the curious craft floating toward the city, but the prank fell flat when a change in the weather forced Branson to land a day early in a field outside London!

What's a hedgehog's favorite snack?

Dill prickles!

$\overline{\quad}$ 10

What's black and white and goes up and down?

A zebra in an elevator!

$\overline{\quad}$ 10

How do you stop dogs from chasing people on bikes?

Give them skateboards!

$\overline{\quad}$ 10

How do snowmen get to work?   On bICICLES!

$\overline{\quad}$ 10

Why do monsters eat metal pins?

It's their staple diet!

___ / 10

Why couldn't the doctor see his patients?

Because he'd lost his glasses!

___ / 10

What has a bottom at the top?

Your legs!

___ / 10

Where do pigs live?

In styscrapers!

___ / 10

What color are hiccups?

BURP-LE!

SEW SNEAKY!

Would you like to spring a morning surprise on your favorite brother or sister?

IMPORTANT! This prank definitely requires some grown-up help and permission!

While your subject is out of the house, raid their drawers for a nice selection of socks and underwear. With a needle and thread, gently join them together with one or two stitches to create a chain of clothes, and then neatly place them back in the drawer.

Next morning, keep a joyful ear to their bedroom door as your bleary-eyed sibling reaches out and grabs a string of socks or a parade of underpants!

WHAT'S THAT?!

A super-easy prank to get your friends staring.

All you do is stand still then look up and point. Wait for a few seconds, then lower your hand and walk on. Then look over your shoulder at the people staring at the sky, wondering what you saw!

Great places to perform this prank include:

the park
a playground
the shopping mall
on a busy sidewalk
the zoo

PRO TIP! Combine your pointing with a look of horror, joy, or confusion to really get 'em looking!

GASP!

What kind of underwear do clouds wear?

THUNDERPANTS!

Try the jokes on your friends then check one of the faces and rate out of ten!

Why did the apple run away?

Because the banana split!

 /10

 /10

Why do comic fans listen to the radio when they're driving?

They enjoy car toons!

Why did the rose go to university?

She was a budding genius!

/10

What happened to the law-breaker who got locked in the freezer?

He became a hardened criminal!

 /10

Why are hairdressers never late for work?

Because they know all the shortcuts!

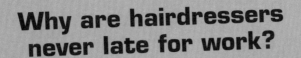

Why did the lady have her hair in a bun?

Because she'd eaten all her burgers!

What did the rock star do when he locked himself out?

He sang until he found the right key!

Why did the elephant miss his flight?

He spent too long packing his trunk!

cereal SWITCH!

What could be merrier than causing mealtime mayhem at the breakfast table?

The night before you spring your surprise, sneak into the kitchen and swap the inside bags of everyone's favorite cereals.

The next morning, step back, play dumb and let the chaos commence!

Where do sick ponies go?

To the horsepital!

What did the man say when he put on a coat made of sausages?

Dinner's on me!

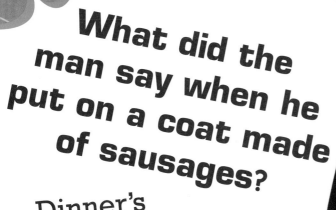

The Australian Iceberg

Everyone was excited when Australian businessman Dick Smith announced that he was going to tow an iceberg into Sydney Harbour. The massive ice mountain was to be broken up into small cubes to sell at 10 cents each, and crowds gathered to see it being towed in. But a rain shower put an end to the prank, revealing the "iceberg" to be nothing but a pile of foam on top of some white sheets!

How do fishermen catch virtual fish?

Online!

Doctor, Doctor, I think I'm a pack of cookies!

Nonsense, you're just crackers!

Whistle while you work!

On April Fool's Day in 2002, the British supermarket Tesco printed a newspaper ad for a specially-produced whistling carrot. This crafty carrot had holes in the side, which would make the veggie blow like a whistle when beautifully boiled!

HONK!

Funny fillings!

Thrill your friends with some dreadful donuts!

Take two filled donuts and carefully make a hole in the bottom of one using the end of a teaspoon handle. Next, squirt a little tomato ketchup or mayonnaise on the end of the spoon handle and push it into the donut. Finally, put both donuts on a plate and offer one to a friend, being careful to take yours first. Enjoy your sweet treat as your friend munches in misery!

HEE-HEE!

What do elves do after school?

Their gnomework!

$2+5=7$

Where do barbers keep their money?

In shaving accounts!

$6 \div 2 = 3$

Why should you always wear glasses to do math?

Because they improve di-vision!

Did you hear about the sad man who lived next to a wall?

He never got over it!

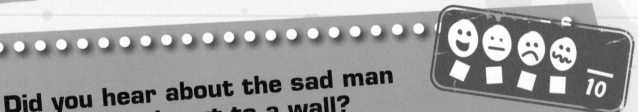

Where do frogs keep their money?

In the riverbank!

Where do crabs keep their money?

In the sandbank!

Did you hear about the man with size 18 boots?

Finding shoes was no small feet!

Did you hear about the man who didn't sit down for 27 days?

He couldn't stand it any longer!

Why doesn't gravity have many friends?

Because it brings everyone down!

frightening fingers

Using a pencil, punch two holes though the Xs.

Wiggle your pencil until the holes are big enough
to put your fingers through.

Turn the page over and put your fingers through the holes.
Close the cover of the book.

Pick your subject and tell them you found something
strange in your book, then open it quickly and
reveal your dreadful digits!

X   X

Aaarrrggghh!

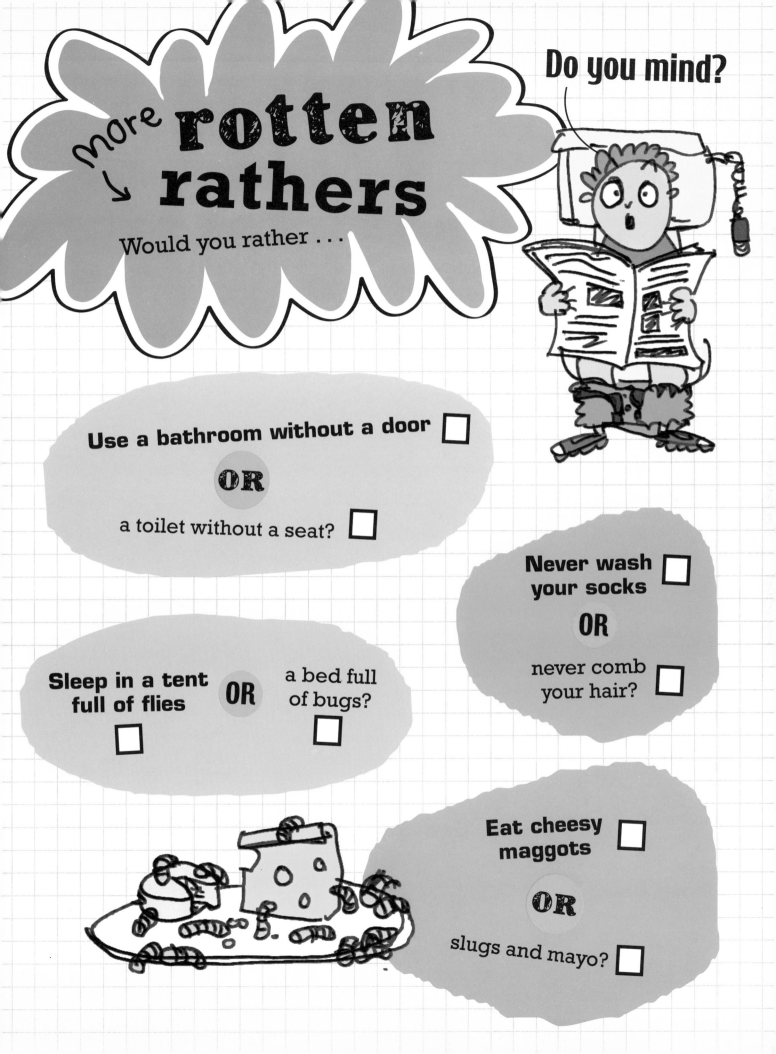

more rotten rathers

Would you rather . . .

Do you mind?

Use a bathroom without a door ☐

OR

a toilet without a seat? ☐

Never wash ☐
your socks

OR

never comb ☐
your hair?

Sleep in a tent **OR** a bed full
full of flies of bugs?
☐ ☐

Eat cheesy ☐
maggots

OR

slugs and mayo? ☐

Excuse-a-pedia

Need an excuse? Try these! If you use an excuse too many times, people won't believe it, so keep track by checking the box every time you use it.

 Oops! I didn't do my homework.

● My little brother stole/ate it!

● Aliens snuck into my room and stole/ate it!

● I had cheese stuck in my ears so I couldn't hear the teacher give the assignment!

 **Oh man, my room is a mess!**

● It's not a mess! It's ART!

● I can't clean because disturbing the dust might upset my allergies!

● It took me weeks to organize my things like this!

● Aliens/my little brother snuck in and messed it up!

3 There is no way I am eating that!

- Point at the window and shout, "What the heck is that?" and while everyone turns to look, drop the offending food into a small bag for trashing later.

- I have a bad reaction to (insert color) food!

- This is so delicious, I must save some (nearly all of it) for (insert name).

- Oh, no, my jaw's stuck! (For this you have to practice talking through your teeth.)

4 What a shame! I can't visit scary Aunt (insert name) because . . .

- I have an unexplained and incurable allergy to her lovely perfume!

- I have an essay to finish, and I really must put my school work before pleasure. (Always impresses.)

- My nice clothes are in the wash and I can't go out without looking my best for Aunt (insert name)!

- I have not been well-behaved recently, so I am grounding myself for a week. Oh, no! That means I can't visit Aunt (insert name)! Well, I'll just have to accept my punishment.

Or, if you just need an excuse, one of these might do the job . . .

The doctor says I must take things easy if there is the letter 'Y' in the day.

I'd love to, but I don't have a clue what you are talking about.

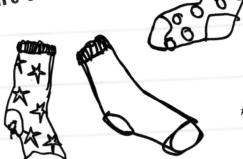

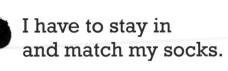

I have to stay in and match my socks.

I have to finish my cheese sculpture.

I have to measure my fingernails.

That would be way more fun than I deserve.

I did do it, but then the cosmos went backwards to a time when I hadn't done it.

I'm saving it as a treat for my 40th birthday.

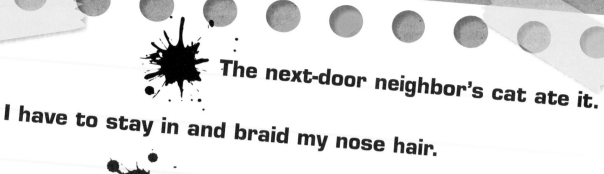

The next-door neighbor's cat ate it.

I have to stay in and braid my nose hair.

I have to knit gloves for my goldfish.

I have to count the contents of a box of cornflakes.

I'd love to, but the TV gets lonely if I leave it alone for too long.

pet rock

I have to stay in and train my pet rock.

I need to catalog my belly button lint collection.

I'm having friends over to watch water evaporate.

I have to lick the salt off my fries.

I have a rare reverse-hearing condition. When you said, "Do," I thought you said, "Don't."

I'm staying in to practice counting backwards from a billion.

Doctor, Doctor, I caught a cold!

Then throw it back, silly!

Achoo!

Doctor, Doctor, I think I'm a train!

Keep on track, and you'll be fine!

real life prank fact . . . real life prank fact . . .

Can Penguins Fly?

Of course they can't! But that didn't stop the BBC from airing a nature show in 2008 showing just that! The program explained that rather than put up with Antarctic winters, the perky penguins flew to the South American rain forests to enjoy the sun. Viewers were amazed to see the waddling wonders soaring through the sky—then later were shown how it was done, with special effects and camera trickery!

TOP **5** USES FOR PLASTIC **CRITTERS**

1. Scatter freely in your sister's underwear drawer.

2. Hide one under the TV remote.

3. Tie to pieces of black cotton and dangle from door frames.

4. Hide them in your friends' shoes.

5. Drop one on your sister's head when she's not looking and see how long it takes her to find it tangled in her lovely locks!

HMMM?

Why did the woman put blush on her forehead?

She was trying to make up her mind!

bedtime beastliness!

Give someone special a bedtime bonus!

Just before bedtime, sneak into your sibling's room and pile some surprises under their sheets. Old shoes, for example, would make a fabulous find, as would a few crunchy cornflakes (be prepared to have to clean them up) or an old frying pan. Make the prank extra memorable by hiding the goodies UNDER the bottom sheet! **Sweet dreams!**

Why was the shirt sad?

Because the jeans were blue!

Why was the belt arrested?

For holding up the pants!

Have you seen the new onion website?

Yes, it's a SITE for sore eyes!

Rotten rathers!

Would you rather . . .

Pour a bucket of slugs over your head . . . or . . . **eat a snail sandwich?**

Sit in a bathtub of snakes . . . or . . . **dye your hair green?**

Run around school in your underwear . . . or . . . **have six school detentions?**

Fill your pockets with cockroaches . . . or . . . **fill your shoes with maggots?**

Lie on a bed of nails . . . or . . . **lie on a bed of worms?**

Drink a cup of bathwater . . . or . . . **drink a cup of pond water?**

DISGUSTING DIGIT!

Creep out your younger sibling with your "spare" finger!

Take a small foam or paper cup with a lid and make a hole in the bottom big enough to stick your finger through. Put the middle finger of either hand through the hole and practice folding your fingers so it looks as though you are holding the cup in the palm of your hand. Put the lid on the cup and carry a book or bag in your other hand. Ask your sibling to open the cup for you (since your hands are full). As they open the cup, wiggle your finger to give them the fright of their life.

"TO BE OR NOT TO BE"

Where do football players eat Thanksgiving dinner?
The supper bowl!

Why did the bottom become an actor?
It wanted a leading fart!

Why doesn't Tarzan need a calculator?

Because the jungle's full of **ADDERS!**

What's yellow and sneezes?

A lemon with a cold!

slippery pencils!

Take a little liquid soap and smear it lightly over the barrels of two or three pencils. Place the pencils on a work surface and challenge a friend to a game of hangman. Offer them a pencil, then join in the fun as they fail to get a grip!

Try the jokes on your friends then check one of the faces and rate out of ten!

Why don't polar bears wear glasses?

Because they have good ice-sight!

 /10

What's green and sniffs?

A cucumber with a cold!

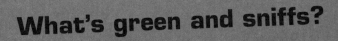

/10

Did you hear about the calendar thief?

He got 12 months!

/10

Why did the boy cover his hands in fertilizer?

He was trying to grow palm trees!

 /10

How did the bicyclist puncture his tire?
He drove over a fork in the road!

What's red and hairy and goes up and down?
A raspberry in an elevator!

What lives underground and uses bad language?
Crude oil!

Why do fleas never pay train fares?
They prefer itchhiking!

itch
itch
itch
itch
itch

flea ville

Why is it hard to talk to a hairdresser?

Because they'll keep cutting you short!

COOKIES 'N' sCREAM!

If filling a donut with a freaky flavor was just too much fun, try this cookie-based caper for more laughs!

Take a selection of sandwich-style cookies and gently open them up. Add an edible (but unexpected) flavor to the cream filling—for example, a sprinkling of salt and pepper or a little mayo—then carefully put the cookies back together. Offer your friends a tasty treat, then watch their faces fall as they sample the terrible taste!

Moving Monument

In 1986, a French newspaper made the shocking—and totally untrue—announcement that the famous Eiffel Tower would be taken down and moved to become an attraction at the new Disney park in Paris!

OOH LA LA!

Why did the man take a clock on the plane?

He wanted to see time fly!

What went through the **window**?

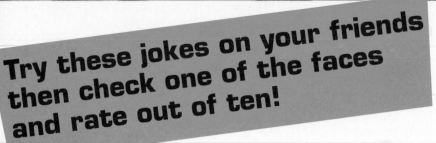

Which animal should you never play with?

A cheetah!

/10

Which vegetables will you find in a closet? Jacket potatoes!

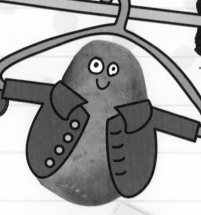

"Doctor, my nose is 11 inches long!"

"Come back if it grows into a foot!"

/10

Why was the archaeologist depressed?

His career was in ruins!

/10

Why did the broom get married so fast?

Because she was swept off her feet!

5 excellent things to do with a **fake booger**

1 Leave it on top of your mom's lovely fresh laundry.

2 Place next to your sister's fork at the dinner table.

3 See if you can make it hang from your nose, then go to school without it falling off.

4 Place it on the palm of your hand, then shake hands with a pal or random relative.

5 Stick one on the side of a packet of cookies, then offer them to a favorite aunt.

What could be worse?

Start in the red box and follow the
arrows, filling in each box as you go.

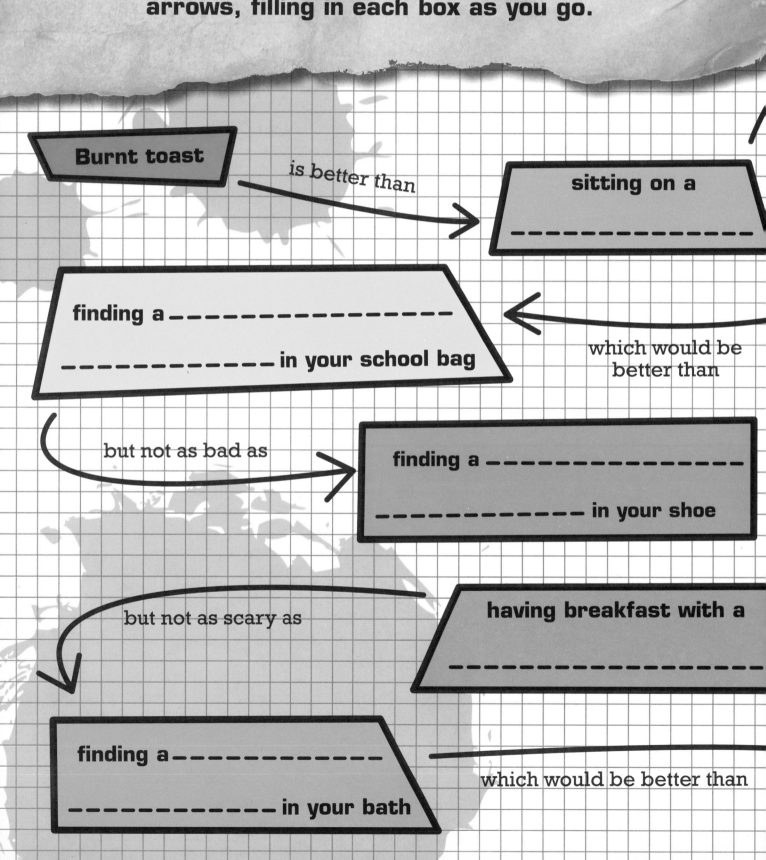

Burnt toast

is better than

sitting on a
_ _ _ _ _ _ _ _ _ _ _ _ _ _

which would be
better than

finding a _ _ _ _ _ _ _ _ _ _ _ _ _ _ _
_ _ _ _ _ _ _ _ _ _ _ _ _ **in your school bag**

but not as bad as

finding a _ _ _ _ _ _ _ _ _ _ _ _ _ _ _ _ _
_ _ _ _ _ _ _ _ _ _ _ _ _ **in your shoe**

but not as scary as

having breakfast with a
_ _ _ _ _ _ _ _ _ _ _ _ _ _ _

which would be better than

finding a _ _ _ _ _ _ _ _ _ _ _ _ _
_ _ _ _ _ _ _ _ _ _ _ _ _ **in your bath**

which is worse than →

sitting in a bathtub of
_____

which is a picnic compared to

going on vacation with a
_____

which would be as gross as →

sharing a toothbrush with a
_____

or

having dinner with a
_____

which wouldn't be as bad as

finding a _____
_____ **in your bed!**

→ **The end!**

Why did the nose hate team sports?

Because he never got picked!

Metric Madness

In 1975, an Australian news show announced that the country would be moving to "metric time." This meant that instead of 60 there would be 100 seconds in a minute and 100 minutes in an hour. To make matters even crazier, there would be 20 hours in a day, seconds would be renamed "millidays" and hours, "decidays." They even showed a new clock with 10 hours on its face!

ALARMING!

There's nothing worse than being woken up when you are having a nice snooze, so why not give a "loved one" (that is, your older sister or younger brother) this treat by hiding an alarm clock in their room? Set the clock nice and early and hide it somewhere they wouldn't think to look. Be sure the clock doesn't have a loud tick or you may be found out!

IT'S ALL ABOUT TIMING!

Why do boiled eggs make good athletes?

Because they're hard to beat!

BLOW soccer

1. Cut out the straws on the opposite page. Roll them up and wrap tape around the ends of each one to hold them together (and stop them from getting soggy).

2. Cut out the goalposts and place them about 8 inches (20 cm) apart at either end of the table.

3. Cut out the ball and scrunch it up.

4. Place the ball in the middle of the table and use your straw to blow it into your opponent's goal.

5. If you want more rules, make them up yourself!

straws

Cut around the dotted lines.

Yes, really, go and get some scissors, **NOW!**

goalposts

ball

YES! More cutting!

Stick a picture of your head here, then draw yourself as the pranking hero you know you are.

Try these pranks and check each one when you've completed it. Then give it a thumbs up if you would do it again or a thumbs down if it was a major fail.

Cereal surprise!

Offer to make your brother or sister breakfast.

Pour some cornflakes into a bowl, then squirt some mayonnaise and ketchup on top.

YUCK!

Then pour some more cornflakes over the top (to hide the sauces) and add milk.

YUCK!

Watch their surprise as they munch on mayo!

Job done!

Cereal surprise 2!

Take the inner bag out of a cereal box and put it somewhere safe.

Fill half of the box with tiny balls of scrunched-up old newspaper.

See the joy on your subject's face as they pour their favorite morning meal!

Job done!

sock SURPRISE!

If you made a few too many newspaper balls (or, hey, even if you didn't, why not make some more?), try sneaking some into your brother's socks.

Push some paper balls into the socks, then neatly fold the socks back and put them in his drawer.

Wait until he takes a pair from his drawer and **LOL** as he wrestles with the rustling socks!

Job done! 👍 👎

just say the word!

This prank works best if you team up with your brother or sister.

Before dinner, pick a word—it must be one that is likely to be used throughout the meal, like **"please."**

Dee-da-da-dee!

Every time your mom or dad says the word, cough really loudly or make a dumb noise.

This is guaranteed to annoy!

Job done! 👍 👎

April Fool's!

Quick and easy pranks for that special day . . .

Achoo!

1. Put a little water in your hand and stand behind your subject. Cough, and flick the water at their neck. **Eeeew!**

Put a little honey on your brother's/sister's breakfast spoon for a sticky surprise!

2.

3. Wear your sweater backwards and act as though nothing's wrong.

4. Sneak into the bathroom and put plastic wrap around the soap!

5. *Birth Certificate*

Tell your friends that your parents found your birth certificate and discovered you're three years older than you thought.

6. Separate your brother's socks and fold them back together in odd pairs.

Hee-hee! Hee-hee!

7. Put a piece of bread on a plate, sprinkle it with water so that it gets soft, then offer it to a friend.

Yuck!

8. Tell your friends that you discovered you were born with green hair and your parents put special medicine in your cereal to make it a "normal" color. See who believes you!

9. Reset your sister's ringtone to something really annoying.

10. Turn the your brother's/sister's alarm clock forwards an hour whilst they're sleeping—for an extra early wake-up call!

Find the difference

What's under the **scary** sofa?

Think of 5 things beginning with...

N _____

A _____

S _____

T _____

Y _____

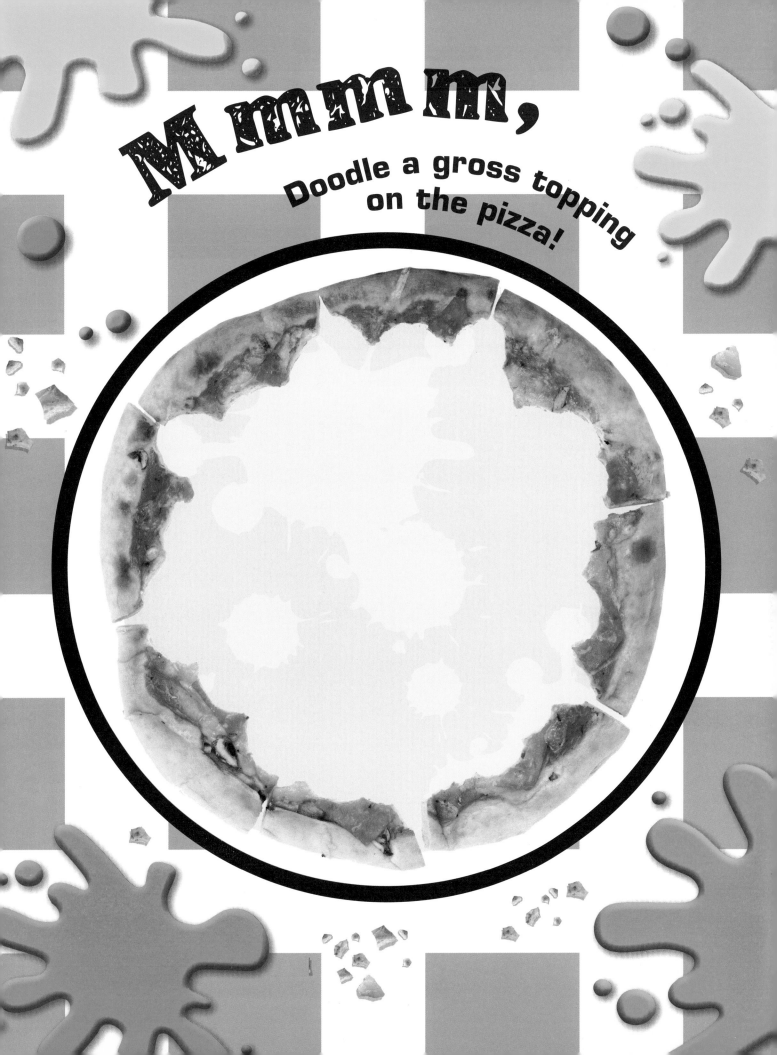

M m m m m,

Doodle a gross topping on the pizza!

Mischievous messages!

Leave a prank note by someone's phone and watch them pick up the message!

Found a great place for our vacation— please call **Candice B. dePlace**

We're out of food— please call **Hammond Egz**

The house is a mess—please call **Dustin D. Furnicha**

Funny messages

Get off the couch!

Stan Dupp

What kind of vegetables do you find in the gym? Muscle sprouts!

Stand up straight!

Denise R. bent

EXCUSE ME!

Why did the tomato blush?

Because he saw the salad dressing!

What's lurking in the loch?

For years, people have believed that a sea monster lives in the waters of Loch Ness in Scotland. In 1972, many thought evidence had finally been found when a huge carcass was seen floating in the chilly lake. This deepwater discovery made the news all over the world, but it soon turned out to be an enormous elephant seal, which had been brought into the waters as an April Fool's joke!

Prank log

Prank name	Who did you prank?	Date	Score (out of 10)

Prank log

Prank name	Who did you prank?	Date	Score (out of 10)

Prank log

Prank name	Who did you prank?	Date	Score (out of 10)

Prank log

Prank name	Who did you prank?	Date	Score (out of 10)

Prank log

Prank name	Who did you prank?	Date	Score (out of 10)